5.18.18

AF081678

KEEP FIGHTING:
Never Give Up
Daily Devotional

DYRANESHEA ROSS

XULON PRESS

*To Theresa,
Always Remember that even in your darkest times where you cannot see the light God is there.
Dyraneshea Ross*

Xulon Press
2301 Lucien Way #415
Maitland, FL 32751
407.339.4217
www.xulonpress.com

© 2018 by Dyraneshea Ross

All rights reserved solely by the author. The author guarantees all contents are original and do not infringe upon the legal rights of any other person or work. No part of this book may be reproduced in any form without the permission of the author. The views expressed in this book are not necessarily those of the publisher.

Unless otherwise indicated, Scripture quotations taken from the Holy Bible, New International Version (NIV). Copyright © 1973, 1978, 1984, 2011 by Biblica, Inc.™. Used by permission. All rights reserved.

Scripture quotations taken from the King James Version (KJV) – public domain.

Scripture quotations taken from the New American Standard Bible (NASB). Copyright © 1960, 1962, 1963, 1968, 1971, 1972, 1973, 1975, 1977, 1995 by The Lockman Foundation. Used by permission. All rights reserved.

Scripture quotations taken from New International Reader's Version (NIRV). Copyright © 1995, 1996, 1998, 2014 by Biblica, Inc.®. Used by permission. All rights reserved worldwide.

Scripture quotations taken from the Living Bible (TLB). Copyright © 1971 by Tyndale House Foundation. Used by permission of Tyndale House Publishers Inc., Carol Stream, Illinois 60188. All rights reserved.

Scripture quotations taken from the Amplified Bible (AMP). Copyright © 1954, 1958, 1962, 1964, 1965, 1987 by The Lockman Foundation. Used by permission. All rights reserved.

Scripture quotations taken from the B. Phillips New Testament (PHILLIPS) The New Testament in Modern English by J.B Phillips copyright © 1960, 1972 J. B. Phillips. Administered by The Archbishops' Council of the Church of England. Used by Permission.

Printed in the United States of America.

ISBN-13: 9781545629260

Dedication

I dedicate this book to my husband and my Pastor, Randolph Ross Jr. It is an honor and pleasure to be married to such an amazing man. I am grateful to God that He allowed you to find me. You are not only my Pastor, but my friend. You give me spiritual guidance filled with the wisdom of God that keeps me on the straight and narrow pathway, which has led to life and life more abundantly. Your love continues to inspire me to reach towards the unseen, knowing that in doing so, I will experience what eyes have not seen and ears have not heard, nor has it entered into the heart of man what God has prepared for them that love Him. Honey, I love you more than words can ever express!

Acknowledgments

I praise God every day for our four children: Randolph Ross III, Khadija Mitchell, Samuel, and Grace Ross. Thank you to each of you for always encouraging me and keeping me on the right track.

To my mother, Gwendolyn Leflore, you have been a great spiritual inspiration to me. Thank you for the prayers, love, words of encouragement, and all the special gifts that you give. You are the best mother in the whole wide world and I am so glad that God allowed me to be your daughter.

To my grandmother, Audrey Mcclendon, you have inspired me in so many ways. As a child, I watched the love and care that you showed towards people. It set a spark within me to love humanity the way that you have done. I watched you show love in deeds and not just in words. You were birthing an amazing blessing within your granddaughter because of your kind and giving heart. It transferred from you to me. I love you so very much, Granny.

To all of my family members who supported this book project, I speak a double blessing on your lives in Jesus' name!

To my wonderful church family, God's House ICF, I love you all! Thank You for all of your support.

To my customers and coworkers, thank you for all of your encouragement, love, and support.

To all my friends far and near, I love and appreciate you all. I am grateful to God for the grace, mercy, and favor that He has bestowed on my life.

Table of Contents

Day 1- God's Plans 1
Day 2–You're Covered! 3
Day 3–The Joy of the Lord 5
Day 4–Breakthrough 7
Day 5–You're Safe! 9
Day 6–Seasons Change 11
Day 7–"I Surrender!" 13
Day 8–Make Your Life Easier! 15
Day 9–Fear Doesn't Have Power to Control You! 17
Day 10–It's Always Going to Be This Way! 19
Day 11–So, You Thought You Wouldn't Make It! 21
Day 12–It's Worth Fighting for! 23
Day 13–Don't Lay Down and Die! 27
Day 14–You Don't Have to Go Down That Road! 29
Day 15–Communicate that You Are a Conqueror! 31
Day 16–Pruning Can Be Painful 33
Day 17–Peace Stealers! 35
Day 18–Don't Get Off Track! 37
Day 19–Relationships Are Important! 41
Day 20–Be Prepared! 45
Day 21–He's Always There! 49
Day 22–Don't Let It Take You Out! 52
Day 23–Draw Closer! 55
Day 24–Keep Your Focus! 57
Day 25–Shame Off You! 61
Day 26–Drop the Baggage! 63
Day 27–Don't Bite the Bait 65
Day 28–Meet Me in the Spot! 69
Day 29–Make God Your Highest Priority! 71
Day 30–Fight Yourself! 73
Day 31–Daddy Was Always There! 77
About the Author 83

Introduction

I am an author and playwright with so much bottled up inside of me that I want to share it with this hurting world. I have learned God has the answer to whatever we are facing in life. This devotional will help guide readers to begin to seek God and study His Word so they can find the answers He offers. Psalm 119:105 says God's Word is a lamp to light our path.

Ronald Reagan, the fortieth President, wrote, "Inside the Bible's pages lie all the answers to all the problems man has ever known. I hope Americans will read and study the Bible. It is my firm belief that the enduring values presented in its pages have a great meaning for each of us and for our nation. The Bible can touch our hearts, order our minds, and refresh our souls."

2 Timothy 3:16 says, "All Scripture is inspired by God and profitable for teaching, for reproof, for correction, for training in righteousness; so that the man of God may be adequate, equipped for every good work" (NASB).

I pray that my readers will heed the words of Psalm 1 so that they may prosper in all they do.

Happy are those who do not follow the advice of the wicked, or take the path that sinners tread, or sit in the seat of scoffers; but their delight is in the law of the Lord, and on his law they mediate day and night. They are like trees planted by streams of living water, which yield their fruit in its season, and their leaves do not wither. In all that they do, they prosper. (Psalm 1:1-3 NRSV)

Day 1
God's Plans

For I know the plans I have for you," declares the Lord, *"plans to prosper you and not to harm you, plans to give you hope and a future.* (Jeremiah 29:11 NIV)

I remember when I had made plans to fly to Indianapolis, Indiana, to visit an old friend. My plans were to spend some quality time with my friend. However, everything went completely opposite of what we had planned. I became a third-leg tagging along with her and her boyfriend. She and I never got to spend any time together. In fact, I was alone much of the time! I wanted to go on that trip so bad that I did not take the time to seek God's will as to whether I should go or not.

When we fail to seek God's plan, we miss out on God's best.

God has great plans for your life. Dwell in His presence today and He will lead you in a path of understanding of His plan for you. Don't allow the distractions of this world to get you side-tracked off His path and follow your own plans. His plan leads you into greatness! Don't be distracted or discouraged, be encouraged!

Read and mediate on God's promise in Jeremiah 29:11.

Pray and ask God to reveal His plan for you today.

Record in your journal what He reveals to you as you dwell in His presence.

Give Him thanks for His plan and ask Him to help you to stay steadfast and not be distracted by life's situations.

Day 2
You're Covered!

The LORD HIMSELF GOES BEFORE YOU AND WILL BE WITH YOU; HE WILL NEVER LEAVE YOU NOR FORSAKE YOU. DO NOT BE AFRAID; DO NOT BE DISCOURAGED. (Deuteronomy 31:8 NIV)

In 2002, we went with a missionary team to the country of Zambia. We were instructed to wear long sleeves throughout the entire trip. The weather there was very hot, yet we were continually instructed to stay covered up so we would not be bitten by mosquitos carrying malaria. While there, we traveled from Zambia to Livingston, an eight-hour drive. On the way, our vehicle got a flat tire and we were stranded. There was absolutely no breeze, so with long sleeves and hot temperatures, I found myself getting physically hot and perspiring heavily.

Throughout the ordeal, I heard the Lord saying, "You are not in this by yourself. I've got you covered! I am God and I am with you. I will never walk away from you. I'm here even when you don't realize that I am here. My eyes go throughout the entire earth beholding the good as well as the evil. If you desire Me, I will come and always be with you to see you through whatever you may be confronted with!"

God is saying this to you today as well.

Read Deuteronomy 31:8 and receive God's promise to you as you go through this day.

Pray and thank God for His promise to never leave you or forsake you.

Ask Him to bring this to your remembrance anytime you begin to get discouraged by life's obstacles.

Record in your journal what He reveals to you as you dwell in His presence.

Day 3
THE JOY OF THE LORD

And do not be worried, for the joy of the Lord is your strength and your stronghold.
(Nehemiah 8:10 AMP)

In this world we have many different types of storms that can cause our vision to become obscured. We have hail storms, rain storms, thunder and lightning storms, wind storms, and snow storms. Each one of these storms can affect the atmosphere in an adverse way. The weather conditions can go from good to bad in the spur of a moment.

In life we will have many different storms that can affect the atmosphere around and within us. A "storm" could be caused by the loss of a loved one, loss of a job, a bad report from the doctor, a failed marriage, or loss of a material item like a home or a car. No matter what form the storm takes, remember God promises strength to get you through it!

In this life, loss is inevitable, but through Christ, loss can always turn to gain!

I want to let you know that you can make it to the other side. These storms may slow you down and cause you to feel discouraged and weak, but don't let them stop you! Get God's Word in your heart and speak what the Word says over your situation.

You have the power through Christ to destroy every evil work of the devil! No matter what storm comes your way today, you can still have the joy of the Lord and the strength to face it!

Read Nehemiah 8:9-12 as an example of this powerful promise from God.

Pray and thank God for giving you strength through Christ to face any of life's storms.

Ask Him to remind you that any loss is gain, and joy is always available through Christ who gives you strength.

Record in your journal what He reveals to you as you dwell in His presence.

Day 4
BREAKTHROUGH

And we know that all things work together for good to them that love God, to them who are the called according to his purpose. (Romans 8:28 KJV)

When we were children back in Biloxi, Mississippi, we would play a game called hide-and-go-seek. The person who was it would close their eyes and count to ten to give everyone a chance to hide. Then they would go seeking to find the hidden players. If he or she found the hidden players, they were eliminated from the game. Then he or she would say to the rest, "Come out, come out wherever you are!" All the other players had to try and run for home base. The person who was "it" was supposed to tag the players before they made it back to home base safely. This person had the power to eliminate the players from the game. A player who remained hidden, though, was automatically eliminated as well and could not continue in the game.

In Genesis we read how Adam and Eve hid from God because they had been disobedient. However, they could not remain hidden. God knew right where they were hiding and called them out of hiding.

Today the Lord is saying come out because I see where you are! It doesn't matter how dark your situation is, He wants you to know He is there to light your way! Your breakthrough is just over the horizon. No matter how dark the day is, know that God has made a way for you to come through to the other side!

Read 1 Corinthians 10:13 and reflect on God's amazing promise to you today.

Pray and thank God for His promise to provide a way out of every temptation you may face in this life.

Ask Him to remind you daily of His desire to light your way and guide your steps to the other side.

Thank Him for the breakthrough He has waiting for you.

Record in your journal what He reveals to you as you dwell in His presence.

Day 5
You're Safe!

God is our refuge and strength, A very present help in trouble. Therefore we will not fear, though the earth should change And though the mountains slip into the heart of the sea; Though its waters roar and foam, Though the mountains quake at its swelling pride. Selah.
(Psalm 46:1-3 NASB)

Here in Florida we have tropical storms and sometimes hurricanes. During those times, the waves of the sea can become very tumultuous and extremely high. If they were to come on shore, they could cause massive damage and destruction. The waves of life can blow you into some hurting places, but remember that you can always run to the arms of the Lord, where there's safety! You're safe in His arms.

Romans 8:38-39 tells us, "For I am convinced [and continue to be convinced—beyond any doubt] that neither death, nor life, nor angels, nor principalities, nor things present *and* threatening, nor things to come, nor powers, nor height, nor depth, nor any other created thing, will be able to separate us from the [unlimited] love of God, which is in Christ Jesus our Lord" (AMP).

Read all of Psalm 46 and apply the truths you read to your present situation.

Pray and thank God for being your refuge and your strength even in the midst of the storms of life.

Ask Him to remind you to run to Him when fear tries to move in.

Record in your journal what He reveals to you as you dwell in His presence.

Day 6
SEASONS CHANGE

Jesus Christ is the same yesterday today and forever more. (Hebrews 13:8 NASB)

We have four different seasons: winter, spring, summer, and fall. In each season, the earth responds differently. In the winter, the grass and the trees which were once green and flourishing, die. In the spring, everything begins to grow and prepares to blossom again. In the summer, everything is green and at full blossom, constantly growing. In the fall, the leaves begin to turn orange, red, and yellow, as the trees lose their leaves. Fall is a time of harvest as well.

Just as there are changes with each of the four different seasons, so is it with life. It's ever changing! As we progress through life, we will begin to grow older. Some of us will experience hair loss, loss of relationships, loss of love ones, and, etc. Some of us will establish new relationships as well. We will also begin to see the fruit of our labor. Through each season of life, we must hold onto God and change and grow as He commands us. Though change isn't always easy, God will be there to see us through.

God is faithful and He will never change because He loves you and He always has your best interest at heart. Do as He asks you to do and you will reap the benefits of your obedience thirty, sixty, sometimes even hundredfold!

Read 1 Corinthians 1:9.

Pray and thank God for His faithfulness.

Ask Him to remind you that He can be trusted and is faithful to fulfill all His promises given in His Word.

Record in your journal what He reveals to you as you dwell in His presence.

Day 7
"I Surrender!"

Thou wilt keep him in perfect peace, whose mind is stayed on thee: because he trusteth in thee.
(Isaiah 26:3 KJV)

All as a kid, my mother would take us to see wrestling matches in the coliseum. The two opponents would wrestle back and forth placing each other in excruciating holds. It would be a back and forth tussle until one or the other was pinned down, gave up, and ultimately lost the match.

There are times within ourselves that we don't seem to find peace. We find ourselves mulling over situations we are confronted with, battling it out within our mind over and over again. As we try to figure out a solution to our situation, we find ourselves running head on in to a mental brick wall. This can ultimately cause massive pain and severe confusion.

Today, I would like to encourage you to stop wrestling within yourself and say, "God, I turn it all over to You. I'm holding on to nothing. I will not pick it back up believing that You may fix my situation. It is too great for me. Lord, I surrender all."

As you do that, you will feel the peace of God instead of confusion and turmoil within you!

Read Philippians 4:7.

Pray and thank God for His promise to give you His peace that is beyond all understanding.

Ask Him to show you how to not only attain but maintain this peace.

Record in your journal what He reveals to you as you dwell in His presence.

Day 8
MAKE YOUR LIFE EASIER!

Now as he traveled on, he came near to Damascus, and suddenly a light from heaven flashed around him, and he fell to the ground. Then he heard a voice saying to him, Saul, Saul, why are you persecuting Me [harassing, troubling, and molesting Me]? And Saul said, Who are You, Lord? And He said, I am Jesus, Whom you are persecuting. **It is dangerous and it will turn out badly for you to keep kicking against the goad [to offer vain and perilous resistance].**
(Acts 9:3-5 AMP emphasis added)

From time to time, I'll encounter people who make statements like, "life is so hard or it's hard to do the right thing!" I've come to learn something about people and life. Anything we make up our mind to do, we will accomplish it and get it done. It often reminds me that God has a destined path for each of us. Whenever we find ourselves constantly meeting trouble after trouble, it is good for us to do a self-survey. In order to do the survey appropriately, we must survey ourselves using the Word of God. The Word of God will allow us to see things about ourselves we would never be able to see on our own! Without the Word of God, we are spiritually blind. For the Word of God is spirit and life! If we're ever going to come through tough times and be the successful people that God has called us to be, we will have to line our lives up with the Word of God.

He's calling you today to let go of your way of doing things so that your life might become easier. Follow Him in faith today, He won't fail you!

Today is the day that you must stop fighting against God and give in to His purpose for your life.

Read and mediate on Acts 9:3-5.

Pray and ask God to reveal how you are fighting against Him and how you can begin to cooperate with His purpose for your life.

Record in your journal what God is instructing you to do then begin to do it!

Give Him thanks for His guidance and purpose for your life.

Day 9
FEAR DOESN'T HAVE POWER TO CONTROL YOU!

For God hath not given us the spirit of fear; **but of power, and of love, and of a sound mind.**
(2 Timothy 1:7 KJV emphasis added)

One of my most frightening childhood memories was when our home was burglarized. It was late one evening after my mother had prepared us all for bed. As we laid sleeping in our beds, I was awakened by my mother's screams. She ran into our room to check on my brother and me. A burglar had broken into our home and stole her watch from her bedside while she slept. His presence woke her and scared her nearly to death! The entire ordeal sparked fear in all of our hearts! We called the police and they came, but my mother wasn't really sure who the burglar was, so she couldn't identify him. We left the house that night, but the very next day we returned. However, we were all very afraid about being in the home and going to sleep. It wasn't very long thereafter that we ended up moving from that home because it had gotten burglarized again one day when we were not home. During that time, God kept us safe. He did not allow the burglar to harm us physically in any way.

There is nothing in your life that you are confronted with today or any other day that will overtake you, because God is there!

Read and mediate on 2 Timothy 1:7.

Pray and ask God to remind you of His promise whenever fear tries to sneak in and control you.

Record in your journal what it means to have a sound mind that overcomes fear.

Give Him thanks for His great and precious promises and His protection over you and your family.

Day 10
It's Always Going to Be This Way!

Why are thou cast down o my soul?
(Psalm 42:11 KJV)

Have you ever found yourself matriculating through life and repeating similar patterns? Have you ever found yourself saying words like, "this is never going to change, or life is always going to be this way?" Well, I have found myself saying things like that in times past.

However, I learned we must come to a place in our walk with Christ that we begin to say what He says! We need to declare His truth over our lives no matter what we see in the natural.

Even though your situation looks completely opposite of what you are declaring, don't stop declaring it! You must see it, say it, and step into it! Things we see with our natural eyes are not what God sees from His perspective. God is omnipresent and omnipotent. The Word of God says He knows the end from the beginning. He is waiting to bless you right now because you've declared what He declares about you and your life.

He is watching over His word to perform it!
(Jeremiah 1:12)

Remember, it's just a process that you must come through. It may look like it's always going to be this way. It may look like you will never change and that things will never change. It may look like an impossible situation, but just when you think all hope was gone, you will find there is hope! Why?

His Word declares, "All things work together for the good of those who love Him" (Romans 8:28 NIV).

Read and mediate on Psalm 42:11, Jeremiah 1:12, and Romans 8:28.

Pray and ask God to strengthen you as you stand on His Word so you can go through the process and change what needs to be changed in your life.

Record in your journal what His Word reveals you should declare over your situation. Then declare it every day until you see it fulfilled in your life.

Give Him thanks for His guidance and encouragement every step of the way toward fulling His purpose in your life.

Day 11
So, You Thought You Wouldn't Make It!

*For with God **nothing** shall be impossible!*
(Luke 1:37 NKJV emphasis added)

Growing up, I met with a lot of difficulties. I was a very troubled young girl and an even a more troubled teenager. I desired to be loved by my father, but unfortunately, I didn't know my father. He was killed in a car crash when I was nine years old. When I found out that he had been killed, it left me in a very sad state.

I found myself beginning to look for love in all the wrong places. I looked for love from man after man and I still couldn't find any fulfillment. I didn't know my value or my self-worth. I never had a male figure in my life to show me how a man was truly supposed to love a woman. It got to the point I felt like my life was taking a downward spiral very fast.

The devil would tell me things like, "You're never going to make it in life and you're not going to be successful." He tried to get me to end my life through suicide because I was so depressed. During these times, I would always talk to God and ask Him to forgive me and help me to change. I really wanted to change. I didn't like the way my life was going.

When I was twenty-three, I decided to give Jesus my life. It was the most rewarding and fulfilling thing that I had ever done. It turned my life around and now my life is complete and fulfilled.

Never count yourself out or a hopeless case. Through Christ, you can become the person God has called you to be!

Read and mediate on Luke 1:37 and Joshua 1:1-7.

Pray and ask God to give you the strength and the courage to face your seemingly impossible situation.

Record in your journal as God shows you how He is the God of the possible!

Give Him thanks that nothing is impossible for Him!

Day 12
It's Worth Fighting for!

Now thanks be to God who always leads us in triumph in Christ, and through us diffuses the fragrance of His knowledge in every place.
(2 Corinthians 2:14 NKJV)

Anything that has value to you is worth fighting for. When my husband and I reached our tenth year of marriage, we begin to meet some difficult times. We had made wedding vows that we would stay together for better or worse, in sickness and health, in wealth and in poverty. My husband lost his job and we were limited on the things that we could do because we had to conserve our resources.

I had been used to living my life the way that I wanted to financially. So, when the money got tight, I didn't like it at all! My husband would do odd jobs, but it wasn't what I was accustomed to him earning. God continued to provide for us through my job and the odd jobs that he worked for the next two and a half years.

During that time, one of my high school male friends began to reach out to me through social media. He had been trying for years to contact me. He was finally successful and we begin to chat every now and then. Soon, we were chatting more frequently, and I found myself becoming very attracted to him.

I was a married woman and I knew that it was wrong, but I just couldn't seem to fight my emotions. He lived five hours away, but then one day my job took me to where he lived. I wanted desperately to see him, so while I was in his city on business, we planned to see each other. One of my girlfriends accompanied me to dinner with him.

When I got home, there was a lot of turmoil in my home because of what I had done. It was not easy to let go of that relationship, but I did! I truly loved my husband and God more than I wanted that outside relationship. I knew my husband was a man who loved God, loved me, and loved his children. He was just in a period in his life where he was trying to discover himself and the path that God had for him. I had so much to lose and nothing to gain by being tempted outside the boundaries of my marriage!

The old saying that the grass is never greener on the other side is so true. I wasn't willing to let go of the great and valuable family that God had given to me. It just wasn't worth it! My husband and I made it through that difficult time in our marriage and we are still together after more than seventeen years.

I learned a very valuable lesson during that time, though. Anything that has value is truly worth fighting for. I love my husband and my children!

The enemy would have liked nothing better than to destroy my marriage and our family.

Jesus warned us in John 10:10, "The thief comes only to steal and kill and destroy" (NASB).

Read and mediate on 2 Corinthians 2:14 and John 10:10.

Pray and ask God to show you how to stand strong and do things His way so that your enemy is defeated, and you are triumphant in Christ.

Record in your journal your struggle, God's help, and your victory in Him.

Give thanks to your loving heavenly Father who brings you the victory in Jesus, your Savior forever!

Day 13
Don't Lay Down and Die!

I have told you these things, so that in Me you may have [perfect] peace and confidence. **In the world you have tribulation and trials and distress and frustration; but** *be of good cheer [take courage; be confident, certain, undaunted]! For* **I have overcome the world. [I have deprived it of power to harm you and have conquered it for you.]**
(John 16:33 AMP emphasis added)

When I first started going to cosmetology school full time, I was also working full time and striving to be faithful to my ministry. It was very overwhelming at times. There were times when I was frustrated with not having the appropriate transportation to get from place to place. I was young, living on my own, and staying in a completely different state from my mother. We didn't have all the low-cost transportation services that we have now. My job and my school were both twenty miles from where I lived. It was sometimes challenging getting back and forth in a timely manner in order to meet the demands of my scheduled activities. There were many days of deep discouragement.

Everything around me seemed to push me to give up and succumb to my circumstances. However, everything within me was saying I should keep going. God encouraged me through His Word assuring me He already had a way prepared for me.

If you don't quit, you are going to reap the reward.

Galatians 6:9 assures us, "Let us not become weary in doing good, for at the proper time we will reap a harvest if we do not give up" (NIV).

Even through those difficult times, I was determined not to quit. Continuing to go and complete my endeavors was one of the best decisions I have ever made. It has indeed been very rewarding.

I want to encourage you to keep going even when everything around you is saying quit and give up. Don't let the demon of discouragement trap you! Keep going! There awaits a great blessing just around the bend. You must press through this difficult time in your life and go get your blessing!

Read and mediate on John 16:33 and Galatians 6:9.

Pray and ask God to give you what you need to not grow weary.

Record in your journal how God's mercy and grace has brought you through your trial and tribulation to reap your harvest and reward.

Give Him thanks for never giving you more than He has equipped you to handle.

Day 14
You Don't Have to Go Down That Road!

The naive believes everything, But the sensible man considers his steps. (Proverbs 14:15 NASB)

Whoever heeds life-giving correction will be at home among the wise. (Proverbs 15:31 NIV)

Whoever gives heed to instruction prospers, and blessed is the one who trusts in the Lord. (Proverbs 16:20 NIV)

When I was a kid back in Mississippi, we used to love when it was honey bee season! One year, we made a game of catching honey bees. We put a sock on one hand and held a jar with the other hand. Once the bee landed on the flower to suck the nectar, we were to catch it and put it in the jar. Whoever caught the most would be the winner.

However, I soon discovered when I swooped down to catch it, the bee stung me right through the sock. It was one of the most painful things I had ever encountered. I remember taking the sock off and running in the house, crying profusely because the pain was so severe.

A few days later, my young uncle decided to try to do the same thing. I warned him not to try to catch a honey bee with a sock on his hand. I tried explaining to him what happened to me when I did it, but he didn't listen. Guess what happened to him?

I learned a lesson from that experience. Not only would I not try and catch a honey bee like that again, I would use my experience to teach others not to make the same mistake I did.

I wanted to learn from my mistake and at the same time help others not to make that same painful choice.

Read and mediate on Proverbs 14:15, Proverbs 15:31, and Proverbs 16:20.

Pray and ask God to help you not only learn from your mistakes, but help others by transparently sharing what you have experienced.

Record in your journal your testimony and be ready to share it when the Lord gives you the opportunity.

Give Him thanks for His great mercy and grace in your life.

Day 15

Communicate that You Are a Conqueror!

Anxiety weighs down the heart, but a kind word cheers it up. (Proverbs 12:25 NIV)

I've always been a very expressive person. Even as a kid, if something was on my mind, I wanted to discuss it. I've never been a person who was good at holding things in that troubled me. I think it is always good to have an outlet. God should be our first outlet because with Him we can discuss anything. Second, we should have someone in our inner circle of friends we can confide in. It is also important to pray and wait on direction from the Lord for the things on our mind that need to be discussed and communicated.

When you have questions with no answers, you need guidance. When you're troubled and need answers, don't just keep things bottled up inside of you. Communication with God and the people He has placed in your life to give you an outlet.

It is also important to remember that our words can affect our attitude toward our circumstances. If we speak defeat, we are likely to fulfill what we have spoken over ourselves. If we declare we are more than conquerors as God has told us He has made us, that is what we will become.

James 3:9-12 warns us about the value of taming our tongues.

With the tongue we praise our Lord and Father, and with it we curse human beings, who have been made in God's likeness. Out of the same mouth come praise and cursing. My brothers and sisters, this should not be. Can both fresh water and salt water flow from the same spring? My brothers and sisters, can a fig tree bear olives, or a grapevine bear figs? Neither can a salt spring produce fresh water. (NIV)

To move forward and conqueror what has been defeating you, you must communicate with your words that you are a conqueror!

Read and mediate on Proverbs 12:25 and James 3:9-12.

Pray and ask God to give you friends that you can openly communicate what is on your heart.

Record in your journal who these friends are and how they are used by God to encourage you to be a conqueror. Also record the words you are going to declare over your situation.

Give Him thanks that in Him you are more than a conqueror!

Day 16
PRUNING CAN BE PAINFUL

After you have suffered for a little while, the God of all grace [who imparts His blessing and favor], who called you to His own eternal glory in Christ, will Himself complete, confirm, strengthen, and establish you [making you what you ought to be].
(1 Peter 5:10 AMP)

I've been through some painful things in my lifetime. There were times when I wondered why life had to be so painful. When we experience pain in our physical body, it is generally an indication that something could be wrong. There are times that we try to avoid dealing with the pain indicators in our body by not giving attention to them. We sometimes ignore them until the pain gets so great that it can no longer be avoided.

All throughout our Christian walk, we try to avoid painful situations. If we could avoid death, suffering, and pain, we would do it no matter what the cost. I've found in my twenty-four years of serving Christ, that in this life we will have tribulations. Pain is unavoidable! Jesus bore excruciating pain on the cross. If there was a cross for Jesus, there will be a cross for you and me to bear as well.

The prayer that I find myself praying every day is, "Lord, help me to endure the things that I must suffer, for Your name sake! In Jesus' name!"

Be encouraged and know that the suffering will only last a short while and will ultimately yield the fruit of righteousness and multiple blessings!

I consider that the sufferings of this present time are not worth comparing with the glory about to be revealed to us. (Romans 8:18 NRSV)

Read and mediate on 1Peter 5:10 and Romans 8:18.

Pray and ask God to help you endure the things you are suffering for His name's sake, knowing they will only last a short while.

Record in your journal the trials you are facing and your determination to see them through to the other side.

Give Him thanks for the strength and endurance He gives you to walk through your wilderness experience, so you can enter your Promised Land.

Day 17
Peace Stealers!

*Peace I leave with you; My [perfect] peace I give to you; not as the world gives do I give to you. Do not let your heart be troubled, nor let it be afraid. [**Let My perfect peace calm you in every circumstance and give you courage and strength for every challenge.**]* (John 14:27 AMP emphasis added)

Have you ever allowed something to steal your sleep and keep you up all night long? Well, I have! I would allow myself to be consumed by a particular situation that I had no control over. Instead of praying and asking God to grant me the peace that I needed to accept the things that I could not change, I allowed it to rob me of my sleep.

As we grow in our relationship with Christ, the Holy Spirit will speak to us about the things that we are supposed to do to attain perfect peace.

No matter what situation you might be confronted with today, I want to encourage you to not let it steal your peace. Rest, relax, and let God revitalize your spirit man today because Christ died to bring you His perfect peace. It's yours, all you have to do is open up your heart and receive it!

Read and mediate on John 14:27.

Pray and ask God to send His Holy Spirit to guide you into that perfect peace.

Record in your journal what the Holy Spirit reveals to you and how you obeyed His guidance.

Give Him thanks for giving you that perfect peace no matter what your situation looks like at the moment.

Day 18
Don't Get Off Track!

A Psalm of David, when he was in the Wilderness of Judah. O God, you are my God, I seek you, my soul thirsts for you; my flesh faints for you, as in a dry and weary land where there is no water.
(Psalm 63:1 NRSV)

It seems that everything around us in the world we live in moves at an extremely fast pace. We have fast moving internet, fast moving cars, and fast-moving people. Everything is downloaded so quickly, it is literally impossible to keep up with it all. You can become so busy trying to keep up with all the technology of this age that it becomes overwhelming.

To be able to process and handle all these things that are being sent your way every day, you must spend time daily with God. It's easy to get off track with the things of God when you spend all your time doing the things of life. The Psalmist wrote, "early will I seek thee, Lord" (KJV).

Jesus left us an example as we read how He went off every morning to spend time alone with the Father, so that He could handle all that would confront Him as He walked through His day (see Matthew 14:23, Mark 6:46, Luke 6:12).

If Jesus felt it was essential to set time apart to be with the Father on a daily basis, how much more important is it for us!

In order for you and me to stay balanced, we must spend time daily with God.

> *May He grant you out of the riches of His glory, to be strengthened and spiritually energized with power through His Spirit in your inner self, [indwelling your innermost being and personality], so that Christ may dwell in your hearts through your faith. And may you, having been [deeply] rooted and [securely] grounded in love, be fully capable of comprehending with all the saints (God's people) the width and length and height and depth of His love [fully experiencing that amazing, endless love]; and [that you may come] to know [practically, through personal experience] the love of Christ which far surpasses [mere] knowledge [without experience], that you may be filled up [throughout your being] to all the fullness of God [**so that you may have the richest experience of God's presence in your lives, completely filled and flooded with God Himself**]. Now to Him who is able to [carry out His purpose and] do superabundantly more than all that we dare ask or think [infinitely beyond our greatest prayers, hopes, or dreams], according to His power that is at work within us.*
> (Ephesians 3:16-20 AMP emphasis added)

Read and mediate on Psalm 63:1, Ephesians 3:16-20, Matthew 14:23, Mark 6:46, and Luke 6:12.

Pray and ask God to fill you with His presence as you spend time daily with Him.

Record in your journal the joy you receive as you spend time in God's presence.

Give Him thanks for allowing you to come into His presence and spend time with Him as He prepares you to meet the challenges of your everyday life.

Day 19

Relationships Are Important!

When David had finished speaking to Saul, the soul of Jonathan was bonded to the soul of David, and Jonathan loved him as himself.
(1 Samuel 18:1 AMP)

I have a friend who has been my friend since fifth grade. Over the years, we traveled down different roads and we even lost contact from time to time. Even during those times, we lost contact, she was always in my heart. My desire was always to get back in contact with her and God allowed us to find our way back to one another. The time that we were separated made us realize how important we were to one another and it made our bond that much tighter. Once we were reunited, we appreciate the relationship even more!

It is important to work on the relationships that God has placed in your life even though relationships sometimes take work. There are some people who think that the can stand alone and be effective. They do everything by themselves. They go to dinner by themselves, they go to the movies by themselves, they go shopping by themselves, and they take vacations by themselves. Don't get me wrong, I'm not saying that there is anything wrong with doing things by yourself. However, people who feel like they do not need anyone because they can handle life on their own are missing out on the joy of a healthy, life-giving relationship.

Life was never meant to be lived alone.

If that was the case, God would have never given Adam, Eve and He would have never have given Jonathan, David. David's testimony before Saul and Jonathan's response to hearing it established a friendship of admiration and loyalty that lasted beyond Jonathan's death (see 2 Samuel 9).

God knew that it wasn't good for man to be alone! Relationships with the right people are good for us spiritually, mentally, emotionally, and physically. God never created us to be alone because He understood that no man is an island. Having healthy relationships helps us to be more what God has called us to be. Healthy relationships can challenge us to stretch in so many different ways. They can bring us out of our comfort zones. Just like David had Jonathan, God has a covenant connection for you.

Don't settle for ungodly relationships that push you further away from Him.

Read and mediate on 1 Samuel 18:1 and 2 Samuel 9.

Pray and ask God to give you that person or people He would have you to be connected to.

Record in your journal how those God ordained connections help you move out of your comfort zone and stretch you to become stronger.

Thank Him for leading you to that covenant connection that will grow and stretch you into the person He has destined you to become.

Day 20

Be Prepared!

Moreover it is required in stewards, that a man be found faithful. (1 Corinthians 4:2 KJV)

Death is a subject that we never want to talk about, but it is inevitable. It's something that we must discuss and prepare for. The greatest preparation of all is making sure that our souls are made right with God through Jesus Christ. The next thing that we should do is make sure that all the necessary arrangements have been made for our funeral. We should never leave the burden of our funeral expenses with our loved ones because it creates a greater hardship for them during their time of grief.

I know that this is a subject that very few people wish to talk about, but we need to be good stewards by having everything in order for the day that the Lord calls us home. Death has no specific age. Only God knows the length of our time here on this earth. Therefore, we must manage the affairs of this life effectively while we are still in these "temples" He has breathed His life into. When we take care of business and properly prepared for our death, we are being the good stewards God has called us to be!

Apostle Paul encourages us with his own testimony of being prepared for his pending death. 2 Timothy 4:6-8 says, "For I am already being poured out as a drink offering, and the time of my departure [from this world] is at hand *and* I will soon go free. I have fought the good *and* worthy *and* noble fight, I have finished the race, I have kept the faith [firmly guarding the gospel against error]. In the future there is reserved for me the [victor's] crown of righteousness [for being right with God and doing right], which the Lord, the righteous Judge, will award to me on that [great] day—and not to me only, but also to all those who have loved *and* longed for *and* welcomed His appearing" (AMP).

Only a man who has been a good steward of the life God called him to could declare he had fought the good and worthy and noble fight. Paul was fully prepared for his death and knew where he was going and what was waiting there for him on the other side.

Are you fully prepared?
Do you know where you are going
and what is waiting for you on the other side?

Read and mediate on 1 Corinthians 4:2 and 2 Timothy 4:6-8.

Pray and ask God to show you what you need to do to be prepared for when He calls you home to be with Him.

Record in your journal the steps you have taken in preparation for your death. Make sure family members know where to find your final instructions.

Give thanks to Jesus for His assurance that He has gone before you to prepare a place for you when your time on this earth is done.

> *Jesus said, "In My Father's house are many dwelling places. If it were not so, I would have told you, because I am going there to prepare a place for you."*
> (John 14:2 AMP)

Day 21
He's Always There!

Teaching them to observe all things whatsoever I have commanded you: and, lo, I am with you always, even unto the end of the world. Amen.
(Matthew 28:20 KJV)

When I gave Christ my life, I was twenty-three years old. Afterwards, I joined a local church where God planted me, and I served there diligently. I was on fire for the things of God. I had a hunger and thirst that just seemed to grow with every passing day. I was not ashamed of my faith and I was more than willing to share Jesus with everyone I met. I almost felt like the woman at the well in the Bible. Everywhere I went, I would invite people to come and see the "man" who have told me everything that I had ever done. I was compelling men and women to come to church with me and I was sharing my faith with others. I was eager for them to get to know the Jesus, the "man" who had forever changed my life.

Throughout my life, many people came to know Christ. While serving in the ministry, I met my husband. We dated for over a year and then married. We served together in ministry faithfully for many years. We were an asset within the body of Christ.

Then God started speaking to our hearts about changing ministries and going somewhere else. He dealt with us for about three years about this change that was coming in our lives and in our ministry. God said our season there was over after sixteen years. We discussed with our leadership what God had given to us. However, he refused to give us his blessing. We had to obey God and left against his wishes.

Once we left, those who were once our friends were not allowed to be in contact with us anymore. We were ostracized. It was a very lonely time in my life being excommunicated from those we had traveled with, prayed with, cried with, and laughed with. People we had relationships with for sixteen plus years were no longer allowed to be our friends. It was such a painful time in my life, but God carried me through.

Obey God because He will lead you to a place of promise. You never know what life will bring, but you can be certain God will be there to comfort, lead, and cover you.

During those times of rejection, God covered us and I got to know God better than ever. I even discovered some new and wonderful things about myself! God used that time to grow and prepare me for the next season of ministry.

**Life can present some lonely paths,
but we are never alone!**

God has said, "Never will I leave you; never will I forsake you." So we say with confidence, "The Lord is my helper; I will not be afraid. What can mere mortals do to me?" (Hebrews 13:5-6 NIV)

Read and mediate on Matthew 28:20 and Hebrew 13:5-6.

Pray and ask God to comfort you during times when obedience to Him affects your relationships with others.

Record in your journal how God Himself comforted you through your lonely times.

Give Him thanks for never forsaking you, for being your helper, and an ever-present companion through every trial of life.

Day 22
DON'T LET IT TAKE YOU OUT!

*I would have despaired unless I had believed that I would
see the goodness of the Lord in the land of the living.*
(Psalm 27:13 NASB)

Some people think that when you are anointed by God, that you are not going to meet opposition. They think that serving God is going to be something easy and something pretty. David was anointed, appointed, and approved by God and it literally brought war to him. In fact, David was anointed to be king over Israel three times. He didn't have to go looking for the fight, the devil brought the fight to him. There was a "hit" on his life.

There is something about being anointed that brings war. It wasn't until David was anointed that the trouble began. As long as David was attending to those few little sheep at his Daddy's house and wasn't causing any damage to the kingdom of the devil, he wasn't meeting that much opposition. Occasionally, he'd meet a little lion or a little bear, but it wasn't like a full out war.

As long as you were doing what you wanted to do and living in the world and not what God called you to do, everything seemed to be going along fine. The moment you decided to obey God and follow His plan for your life, you began to meet opposition on every side. The children started acting up, the teenagers started tripping out, your spouse started acting crazy, and loneliness and depression were at an all-time high in your life. Then you were laid off work, a loved one died, you received a back-tax notice from the IRS, and got a bad report from the doctor.

That's when you **must not** be confused by all the fiery darts of the enemy and know that you are right smack dab in the will of God! God is with you, God is for you, God is on your side.

David was harassed by Saul and distressed by the Amaliktes, but he believed he was going to see the goodness of the Lord in the land of the living.

Have you ever had a situation in your life that kept harassing and distressing you? It seemed that everywhere you turned trouble was there picking on you? Well, let me encourage you today to remember all the things God has brought you through many times before. You must be like David and believe that you will see the goodness of the Lord in the land of the living. Whatever you do don't stop fighting because this is not the time to quit. You must believe the promises of God are for you!

What you believe is what you will receive.

Read and mediate on Psalm 27:13.

Pray and ask God to remind you of all the things He has already brought you through.

Record in your journal what you believe and then document what you receive.

Give Him thanks for He is faithful to do what He has promised He will do.

Day 23
Draw Closer!

Draw nigh to God, and he will draw nigh to you. Cleanse your hands, ye sinners; and purify your hearts, ye double minded. (James 4:8 KJV)

I remember when my husband and I first starting dating, I was so excited. I always looked forward to being in his presence. I couldn't wait to see him and be with him. The anticipation of being in his presence made me so excited. Whenever he would call, I would be so happy. I could feel the happiness in my soul! What I felt in my soul was directly connected to my facial expression. My face was so full of joy, I would be smiling from ear to ear. With every fiber of my being, I wanted to be close to that man and he wanted to be close to me. Our level of intimacy grew closer each time we talked or spent time together. It was our desire to draw closer to one another through marriage.

God is saying it is time to draw closer to Him. He says it's time to get into His presence. He can make your spirit feel the joy that it may have never felt. The more that you move into His presence, the more that you will see things in your life transform. The more that you get in His presence, the more you crave and thirst for Him. He wants to fill you up with His Spirit and bring your heart joy.

Let Him in and draw close!

Read and mediate on James 4:8.

Draw close to Him and rest in His wonderful presence!

Record in your journal the joy you experience in His presence and the way He is transforming your life.

Give Him thanks for His love and for filling you with His Spirit and joy.

Day 24
Keep Your Focus!

Therefore, since we are surrounded by so great a cloud of witnesses [who by faith have testified to the truth of God's absolute faithfulness], stripping off every unnecessary weight and the sin which so easily and cleverly entangles us, let us run with endurance and active persistence the race that is set before us, [looking away from all that will distract us and] focusing our eyes on Jesus, who is the Author and Perfecter of faith [the first incentive for our belief and the One who brings our faith to maturity], who for the joy [of accomplishing the goal] set before Him endured the cross, disregarding the shame, and sat down at the right hand of the throne of God [revealing His deity, His authority, and the completion of His work]. Just consider and meditate on Him who endured from sinners such bitter hostility against Himself [consider it all in comparison with your trials], so that you will not grow weary and lose heart.
(Hebrews 12:1-3 AMP)

I remember when I was in high school and I was running track. I would be either the second or third leg of the relay team. Whenever we were in the midst of the race, it would always be so tempting to look back to see how far away or how close to us our opponent was. Was she gaining on us or were we leaving her in our dust because we were running so fast! When competing in a race it is always important to keep your eyes straight ahead. Anytime you're running and you look back, it takes away your momentum and slows you down. Our goal was to stay focused on the finish line and push our bodies as hard as we could in order to obtain the prize. First place! Focusing on anything other than the finish line was a distraction.

As Christians, we have an opponent whose job it is to get us off track and cause us to focus on our life situations. He is a thief and a liar. His goal is to distracts us little by little and subtlety get us to lose our focus. It is very important that we don't become distracted by the issues of life, such as the baby being sick, the bills being due or us being laid off our job. God is our source and in Him is every resource that we need. If we practice the principles of His Word and allow them to come alive in our life through our consistent relationship with Christ, we can run this race called salvation and not be tempted to quit. It is through our steadfast and immovable relationship with Christ that we have the victory!

Build your relationship with Christ and don't be distracted by the trickster of this world!

Read and mediate on Hebrews 12:1-3.

Pray and ask God to guide through the obstacles that would distract you and take your focus off Him.

Record in your journal when you are tempted to quit and how God helps you run the race and gain the victory.

Give Him thanks that no matter what the trickster tries to pull. God's presence in your life gives you what you need to finish the race and cross the finish line.

Day 25

SHAME OFF YOU!

Purge me with hyssop, and I shall be clean: wash me, and I shall be whiter than snow. (Psalm 51:7 KJV)

You were not created to know shame, guilt, sin, or condemnation. In the Garden of Eden, Adam and Eve would have never known shame if they had not committed the sin of disobedience. Once sin was on board, the eyes of their understanding were popped open.

Like Adam and Eve, I was innocent until I was victimized at a very early age. The enemy targeted me, and I was nearly molested at the age of four. I still remember the incident as though it was yesterday. Through that ordeal and growing up through disfunction and seeing abuse all around me, created a spirit of shame and embarrassment in my life. I always thought that there was something wrong with me. I would say, "If there is nothing wrong with me, then why would those ungodly things happen to me?" It created a spirit of low self-esteem and rejection within my soul.

It also left an open portal for perversion and abuse to enter into my life and my soul. It was there until I opened up my heart to receive Jesus Christ as my personal Lord and Savior. He filled me with the power of His Spirit and began to purge all of the filth, shame, and embarrassment of my past out of my spirit.

No matter what has happened in your past, God is ready to receive you and enter into your heart through the power of His Spirit and wash you as white as snow.

> **Open up your heart and say,
> "Lord, I release it and I'm letting it all go
> that You might come into my heart
> and make me completely whole."**

Read and mediate on Psalm 51:7.

Pray and ask God to wash you and make you whiter than snow, so you can release the bondage of your past.

Record in your journal the joy you feel as you turn all your shame and guilt over to Him and He shows you what a masterpiece you are in His sight.

Give Him thanks for the power of His Spirit that fills you with His love and covers you in His mercy and grace.

Day 26
Drop the Baggage!

Cast thy burden upon the LORD, and he shall sustain thee: he shall never suffer the righteous to be moved. (Psalm 55:22 KJV)

Have you ever flown on a plane and kept your carry-on luggage, lap top, and your hand bag with you as you waited to board your plane? Your bags eventually became heavy and began to weigh you down as you traveled through the airport to the door where you were to board your flight. By the time you arrived at your seat, you were exhausted. Carrying extra baggage can be very taxing. Your body experiences great relief once you drop the baggage.

As we go through life, if we carry a lot of unnecessary, excessive baggage, it weighs us down. It can literally make us sick or even cause death.

Think about the baggage that you take on a trip and how it weighs you down. Imagine the things in life that you are holding on to and do not want to let go. They're heavy and could weigh you down. If you continue to carry them, it could really have a major impact on not only your physical but your emotional and spiritual life as well.

Casting all your cares [all your anxieties, all your worries, and all your concerns, once and for all] on Him, for He cares about you [with deepest affection, and watches over you very carefully].
(1 Peter 5:7 AMP)

The J. B. Phillips New Testament says, "You can throw the whole weight of your anxieties upon him, for you are his personal concern."[1]

God is saying drop the baggage and take up His way and He will lift your heavy burdens off of you.

Read and mediate on Psalm 55:22 and 1 Peter 5:7.

Pray and ask God to show you what unnecessary, excessive baggage you are carrying that He wants to take off of you.

Record in your journal what God has shown you and then release it to Him.

Give Him thanks for lifting your heavy burdens, anxieties, worries, and concerns and carrying them for you. Rejoice at the freedom you feel after giving Him all of your burdens.

---

[1] J.B. Phillips New Testament (PHILLIPS) The New Testament in Modern English by J.B Phillips copyright © 1960, 1972 J. B. Phillips.

Day 27
Don't Bite the Bait

> ***No** temptation [regardless of its source] has overtaken or enticed you that is not common to human experience [nor is any temptation unusual or beyond human resistance]; but God is faithful [to His word—He is compassionate and trustworthy], and He will not let you be tempted beyond your ability [to resist], but along with the temptation **He [has in the past and is now and] will [always] provide the way out as well, so that you will be able to endure it [without yielding, and will overcome temptation with joy].***
> (1 Corinthians 10:13 AMP emphasis added)

Growing up in Biloxi, Mississippi, was an awesome thing. It was a beautiful place surrounded by water. As a child, I would watch fishing and shrimping boats come in and out on a daily basis. It was a very exciting to watch the fishermen bait their hooks to lure the fish in and catch them.

Just as the bait was alluring to the fish, so was the water alluring to us as kids. Time and time again we were instructed by our parents not to go near the back bay or the beach without adult supervision because none of us could swim. There were things that our parents warned us to stay away from because they knew that those things were not good for us and could be harmful to us. However, some of the things our parents told us to stay away from looked attractive and very alluring in our minds.

We did not understand it was the bait Satan was using to lead us to a place of destruction.

One day, we decided to go to the back-bay fishing pier. Unbeknown to our parents, we had gone there many times before and would take turns swinging and dangling off the pole that swung out over the water. We loved the exhilaration and none of us had ever fallen into the bay, but on this particular day one of our friends fell in. None of us in our group knew how to swim, so we could not rescue him! We thought he was going to drown! There were some other kids there who were jumping off the pier into the deep waters. They knew how to swim. They were angels sent by God.

When our friend fell into the water, they realized he could not swim and did not hesitate to jump in and save him. That day his life was saved! We had been instructed by our parents countless times to stay away from the beach and stay away from the bay, but we allowed temptation to get the best of us. I am so glad that God watched over us that day and sent those other children to be there as His special rescue angels.

Remember, whatever bait that the devil may be dangling over your life today, you don't have to bite it! It could be someone else's spouse, but don't bite it! It could be a fine individual of the opposite sex, who wants to sleep with you and you're not married, but don't take the bait! It could be the bait of a same sex relationship, don't bite it! It could be cheating on your taxes, and though the enemy says everyone is doing it, don't bite it! It could be the bait of fear, doubt, or unbelief, but God says you have the power to resist it!

Through every temptation, God has made a way of escape for you. Just make sure that you take the exit door that He has prepared for you. He will close it and lock it behind you. Go through it and don't look back. God has got your back!

Read and mediate on 1 Corinthians 10:13.

Pray and ask God to show you immediately when Satan is trying to lure you into temptation.

Record in your journal how God makes a way for you to avoid the temptations and the bait Satan dangles before you.

Give Him thanks for the victory over every sin and temptation Satan tries to use to lead you to destruction.

Day 28
MEET ME IN THE SPOT!

And ye shall seek me, and find me, when ye shall search for me with all your heart.
(Jeremiah 29:13 KJV)

We all have a place that we call "our spot." It's the place where we find peace and relaxation. It's the place where we can go to clear our head and release all of our cares. It's a place where we find hope and restoration. It is a place where our brokenness is made whole. It is that certain spot where we meet God. It's a place where we don't take anyone else. It's our secret place called our "sweet spot."

Trust [confidently] in Him at all times, O people; Pour out your heart before Him. God is a refuge for us. (Psalm 62:8 AMP)

This is the place where you meet God and turmoil is turned into peace. It's a place where you can let your hair down and can tell God anything. God is ready to take you from the pit to the palace. He's waiting for you to draw closer to Him, so He can be your shelter in the storm.

"I would hurry to my refuge [my tranquil shelter far away] from the stormy wind and from the tempest."
(Psalm 55:8 AMP)

He said in His Word that when you seek Him with all of your heart, it is then that you will find Him. Open your heart today and begin to worship Him and watch how God will shift you from your place of anxiety, worry, and hurt to a place of peace, joy, and healing. That's what happens when you get in that special spot every day and meet Him there.

The devil cannot touch you when you have drawn close to the Lord and met Him in that special spot.

For You have been my help, and in the shadow of Your wings [where I am always protected] I sing for joy. (Psalm 63:7 AMP)

Read and mediate on Jeremiah 29:13 and Psalm 63:7.

Pray: *But as for me, it is good for me to draw near to God; I have made the Lord G*OD *my refuge and placed my trust in Him, That I may tell of all Your works* (Psalm 73:28 AMP).

Record in your journal what you share with the Lord as you praise and worship Him in your secret spot!

Give Him thanks for being your refuge no matter what is going on in your life.

Day 29
MAKE GOD YOUR HIGHEST PRIORITY!

Delight thyself also in the LORD; and he shall give thee the desires of thine heart. (Psalm 37:4 KJV)

In today's society, we have different classes of mail. We have priority, first class, etc. Each class of mail has a time frame in which the mail will be delivered and the price that you pay. In life, we have many priorities—our family, our jobs, and our homes just to name a few. There are certain things that we deem to be our highest priorities. To some of us our families are our highest priority, but to others our job may be our highest priority.

But first and most importantly seek (aim at, strive after) His kingdom and His righteousness [His way of doing and being right—the attitude and character of God], and all these things will be given to you also. (Matthew 6:33 AMP)

I don't know what you value in your heart to be your highest priority, but I pray that it is your relationship with God through Christ. If you place that relationship in its proper place as first in your life, He will cause all of your other relationships to be successful and to soar! Spend time with God each day sorting through the mail of your heart to place your relationships in their proper perspective. As you put God first, watch the power of His goodness be made manifest in each and every relationship that you have established.

As you put Him first, there is no limit to your blessings! He knows your desire, so delight yourself in Him!

Read and mediate on Psalm 37:4 and Matthew 6:33.

Pray and delight yourself in Him as you seek His kingdom and His purpose for your life.

Record in your journal as God lovingly gives you the desires of your heart.

Give Him thanks and praise Him for the many blessings He has bestowed upon you.

Day 30
FIGHT YOURSELF!

There is something else deep within me, in my lower nature, that is at war with my mind and wins the fight and makes me a slave to the sin that is still within me. **In my mind I want to be God's willing servant, but instead I find myself still enslaved to sin.** *So, you see how it is: my new life tells me to do right, but the old nature that is still inside me loves to sin. Oh, what a terrible predicament I'm in! Who will free me from my slavery to this deadly lower nature?* **Thank God! It has been done by Jesus Christ our Lord. He has set me free.**
(Romans 7:25 TLB emphasis added)

Have you ever talked yourself out of doing something you knew you were supposed to do? Have you ever talked yourself out of believing something that you know you were supposed to be believing? Don't be so quick to tell yourself what you cannot do. If we are not prayerful and careful, you will talk yourself right out of your blessing.

I can do all things *[which He has called me to do] through Him who strengthens and empowers me [to fulfill His purpose—I am self-sufficient in Christ's sufficiency;* ***I am ready for anything and equal to anything*** *through Him who infuses me*

> *with inner strength and confident peace.]*
> (Philippians 4:13 AMP emphasis added)

Remember that you can do whatever God has told you to do! You can do all things through Christ who strengthens you! Sometimes, it's easier to believe for others than for yourself, but your best days are ahead of you and your worst days are behind you!

Apostle Paul recognized that he had two members warring within him. One of good, (focused on God). One of evil (focused on the flesh). He was willing to fight to keep the evil desires of his flesh crucified so that the good of Christ's purpose might live on through Him!

Fight yourself! Bring the desires of your flesh under subjection to Christ's Spirit residing within you.

> *Since, then, you have been raised with Christ, set your hearts on things above, where Christ is, seated at the right hand of God.* **Set your minds on things above, not on earthly things.** *For you died, and your life is now hidden with Christ in God. Put to death, therefore, whatever belongs to your earthly nature: sexual immorality, impurity, lust, evil desires and greed, which is idolatry. You used to walk in these ways, in the life you once lived.* **But now you must also rid yourselves of all such things** *as these: anger,*

> *rage, malice, slander, and filthy language from your lips. Do not lie to each other,* **since you have taken off your old self with its practices and have put on the new self, which is being renewed in knowledge in the image of its Creator.**
> (Colossians 3:1-3, 5, 7-10 NIV emphasis added)

Read and mediate on Romans 7:25, Philippians 4:13, and Colossians 3:1-3, 5, 7-10.

Pray and ask God to strengthen and empower you to fulfill His purpose and do all that He asks you to do.

Record in your journal what God has asked you to do for Him and how He has empowered and equipped you to fulfill that purpose.

Give Him thanks for all His many precious promises to you.

Day 31
Daddy Was Always There!

As a child, I spent a lot of time at my grandparents' house. My mother was a single parent who worked quite a bit to provide for me and my two brothers. I am grateful to God for the mother that I had. She did the best that she could to raise us to be productive citizens in life. As a young girl, I could remember my mother taking us to church. Through our church attendance, we begin to learn about Christ.

Having my mother in my life was a great blessing. However, something was lacking in her life. I didn't realize back then how not having my father in my life was going to impact me. My mom did a great job, but could never take the place of my Dad. At twelve years old, I became intimate with a boy. I wanted to be loved, cared for, and made to feel important. I wanted to know that I was beautiful. As I grew older, I found myself in and out of different relationships with men. I was still seeking the affection, approval, and appreciation I had not received from my daddy.

God has designed the family to consist of the father and the mother to raise and care for their children. Any time the father or the mother is missing from the relationship of the family, it creates a sense of brokenness. The family is incomplete. Not having my father in my life created a big gaping hole within my soul! Many days I would wake up in the morning crying and depressed because I didn't know who my daddy was. I didn't realize by not having my father in my life left me vulnerable to preying men. Any man that gave me the least bit of attention, I was his.

I didn't realize my value or my worth because I wasn't connected to Christ. When I truly opened my heart to Christ, He filled that void and healed me. I will not tell you that it happened over night. It has been a process. The spirit of sexual lust within me was so great, that it could only be destroyed through the washing of God's Word and the indwelling of His Holy Spirit. The young woman who was looking for love in all the wrong places, finally found it once she opened her heart and received Christ. Depression, inadequacy, the spirit of rejection, and low self-esteem no longer had the power to imprison me! Christ set me completely free!

> **There will never be a person, place or thing that can heal the brokenness in your soul. Only God!**

To the Prodigal Son or Daughter:

On this thirty-first day of this devotional, I would like to speak to the singles who are in Christ. As a single Christian, it is very important that you get to know yourself and your God very well. It is imperative that you spend time with Him, listening to Him as He's teaching you to learn about yourself. He says in His Word that His children know His voice and a stranger they will not follow (John 10:14-16). You will have all kinds of voices calling for you to enter into ungodly relationships, but let me encourage you to get to know the voice of your Good Shepherd!

God, your heavenly Father, says you are worth more than diamonds, gold, and precious rubies. There is no amount of money in this world that could determine your worth! You are fearfully and wonderful made. When God created you, He hand carved a masterpiece. You can never be duplicated nor imitated, because you are authentic.

You may have had a lot of struggles throughout your lifetime. It may have been very difficult for you to see your value and worth. You may not realize how precious you really are, so you constantly tread through the rough waters of relationship after relationship which can be very tiring. After each ungodly relationship, you find a piece of your soul being torn away from you and a portion of the other individual's soul being deposited within you. God knew the power of sex and the bond that it would bring and that's why He said that it was to be between a man and his wife.

I don't know what road in life you've come down. You could have been raped by your father or some other family member or so-called friend. You could have been abandoned by your mother or both parents. You could have been placed up for adoption or in a foster care system and never knew who your parents were. Your mother could have died when you were young, or you could have been fatherless and felt abandoned. Whatever your situation was, even though it didn't seem like it then, your heavenly Daddy was always there! Our Daddy is able to heal every ounce of hurt and brokenness.

I was a woman who knew no hope. However, when I opened my heart, received Jesus Christ, and allowed Him to come in, He begin to fill every crater, crack, and pot hole in my soul with His love. Every place where sin had left a crimson stain, God began to wash me until I was whiter than snow.

I don't care where you are in life right now, you are not in too deep that God cannot reach down and pick you up. You can be a stripper on the pole in the club or a prostitute on the street, but your heavenly Daddy is there waiting to clean you up! You can come to Him. He is waiting with His arms open wide to wash you, heal you, fill you, and make you whole. He loves you and He is here waiting for you right now to let Him in.

I want to encourage you to get in a good Bible teaching church and ask how you can serve. Get connected with your Pastor and the other congregants that you might grow. If you do, your life will make a 180-degree change and you will live your best life yet!

**God loves you and is always here,
waiting for you to turn to Him!**

And he arose, and came to his father. But when he was yet a great way off, his father saw him, and had compassion, and ran, and fell on his neck, and kissed him. (Luke 15:20 KJV)

Read the parable of the Prodigal Son Jesus told in Luke 15:11-24.

What was the father doing while his prodigal son was out in the world doing his own thing?

How did he treat his son when he returned?

Who did this father represent?

How has this encouraged you to overcome your past?

About the Author

Dyraneshea Ross is an author and play writer. She developed a love for writing about twenty-four years ago. She has written over twelve plays and skits. Her primary goal is to give to this world the gift of drama and writing which was given to her by God. Her heart's desire is to reach this world for Christ through various forms of creative arts such as, writing, drama, and movies.

CPSIA information can be obtained
at www.ICGtesting.com
Printed in the USA
FSHW04n1601120418
46815FS

ISBN 9781545629260